David Kimmeran

Aleman

Introduction

During the past few years we have been threatened with bombs, knife crime, gun totting idiots and politicians with a gung-ho attitude to life. The one thing however that has brought us all, the world to its knees is the Coronavirus or Covid-19. Certainly, on a personal level I never imagined for a second that our lives would suddenly become a scene from a disaster movie. Was the world ready, who knows? We have all been ordered to stay in for our own and others safety and of course to wash our hands whilst singing Happy Birthday.

So as part of my isolation and with my friends on Facebook I have started the above named, what do you call a blog on Facebook, a flog?
Add in some poetry and photography along the way and bang!!

Professionally I call myself 'The Bearded Poet' so, and not in any chronological order, I invite you to sit back and enjoy..........

Isolation Now
and
Adventurer's back then

Mumbles Light-House

These are memories and opinions that are mine alone. There is no offence intended and if anything factually is out, it is how I remember.

Part 1

As a small kid Mayhill was top of the world. From behind the round school I look over parts of Mount Pleasant down further to Hafod and then the mighty Kilvey Hill, which at the age of 6 was bigger than Everest ever could be. I could walk around the bank over and through bushes and with Paul Leonard and David Harris find ourselves on top of the Black Road. Our world was one of adventure, after running down the Black Road we could even travel into outer space whilst playing in the Rocket Park. There were streams to splash in, trees to fallout of and grass areas where Swansea City won the football World Cup every night. There was no playing left to right, it was uphill or down. If you played downhill and kicked the ball to hard it was a run down the Black Road for the ball, if you played up hill there was a good chance you would end up in the stingy nettles. My mother always said I took home half the pitch on my trousers every night.

The 'Green' was a flat patch of grass sitting on the junction of Creidiol Road, Nicander Parade and Place and sloping off to the Black Road and fields, bushes and all sorts of tundra that eventually took you past the stream to North Hill and the Rocket Park.

The 'Green' as it was called, was our football pitch, our wrestling ring and the odd Olympic Games were staged there too. It was our film set where many Star Wars story was rein acted with me as Darth Vadar, David Harris was Luke Skywalker and Mark Sheldon took the role of Chewbacca. As you can imagine the story lines were quite short.

In 1984-5 the Council decided that Mayhill was due a facelift and all the council owned housing were going to be modernised. This meant central heating, gas fires and a fresh lick of paint. It also meant our beloved 'Green' became the storage area and car park for the Council's equipment and vehicles. Even though by now we were teenagers more interested in chasing girls rather than a football it was still uncomfortable seeing our hallowed pitch treated like this.

Growing Pains

As the coloured glass marbles role down the hill
The little boy laughs and runs
There was Apache Joe and the Cowboy Kid,
Hands teetering over plastic guns

A strong breeze brings the smells
Of Swansea to this childish friend
And always with bravery and attitude
They are warriors until days end.

"Ow!, he punched me, Ow he kicked "
Crying and laughing as noses are picked
"My Dad can fight your Dad!" they angrily say
But soon all forgotten continuing to play.

"See that tree, the one down in the park?"
"That's where I kissed Jane, on the lips, in the dark!"
"What was it like, did it taste funny?" they snigger
"Don't know about the taste, but my willy got bigger!"

My word how they laughed these innocent boys
Soon to forget all their games and their toys
Soon they will grow up and be handsome, tall men
No more playing Tarzan or building a den.

Soon comes a day when all kids make you cry
And soon comes the day when they tell you goodbye
But I have been lucky, my daughters the best I could have had
And as for me, I think I'm a pretty cool Dad!

Part 2

Mayhill school was our home for four years. The magnificent D-shaped building was called the round school because looking at the school from a distance the curved aspect of the school gave the impression of being round. The centre of the school saw a small grassy area where I saw one friend being dragged along by his hair by the head master kicking and screaming. The school yard was our football pitch and depending on which school year you were in decided how much of the yard you had to play in. The girls stood around the edges of the yard with skipping ropes and imitations of the latest pop group. The views behind the school breathtakingly took in the docks and industrial areas to the left as you looked and our beautiful beach, the town centre then on to the brilliant Mumbles lighthouse to the right. The clouds dramatically framed the beautiful City we called home

On a personal note Mayhill Junior School for me was horrible. I was overweight, I wore glasses and my middle name of Kimmeran was shortened to Kim so I was bullied, especially by one particular lad. I would offer to help the teacher tidy after school so I didn't have to leave at the same time as him, but then I became teacher's pet so another reason to bully me. I forget by whom but one birthday I was given a £1 note, which back in the late 1970's you could buy quite a lot with. I gave it to him just so I could leave school and walk home without worry. It lasted for a couple of days only. The most powerful part however wasn't any violence that may or may not have taken place, it was the threat, simply the threat.

Maerdy Mountain

As I suggested in the introduction, I am doing this as with so many others in the world today from an isolated world at home. The Coronavirus has taken 105,000 lives worldwide and there are an estimated 2 million people affected. So the world leaders are correct in shutting the world down to prevent the spread and hopefully slow the transmit ion of the disease to a level where it could be controlled.

The only acceptable 'legal' reasons for leaving your home are Essential food and Medication's and an hour of exercise once a day. With people you live with ONLY. Yet I'm sat here on Easter Saturday at 2pm, the sun is blazing down, there is rubbish on TV and people are bored and I will guarantee there are people out in groups today in parks, or down by a river playing or just having friends around for a BBQ.

This is not going to get any better whilst people are saying "I'm carrying on with my life without change".   No! You, me, all of us we have to change, we have to change everything we do in order to stop the spread.

Emrys Jones

Emrys sits on the bench tonight
Thinking of Elsie his love
Painting a memory in his mind...
Together fitting as a glove

He visited her everyday
Whilst longing for her to live
Waiting for her instructional list
And the orders that she give

Married for 37 years
Through babies, through heartache and through verse
Growing up as the clergy man said
For better or for worse

She nursed him coughs ,He nursed her colds
Together they were a team
Sitting now on this lonely bench
For Elsie he can only dream

It seems so wrong, didn't people care?
He cries now as he waits for the bus
If only people had stayed at home
At the outbreak of Coronavirus?

People were asked to stay at home
It got to a point when they were told
And all because they ignored common sense
It took his love because she was old.

So I ask you now and I ask you once
Please stay at home for us all
For Emrys, for me, for your Mam and the world
Going out invites mankind to fall.

Swansea Bay

Part 3

    My daughter and her peers these days can't walk 500 yards without a lift. Back then we walked everywhere. From the Black Road if lucky enough to have any money on the way to school I would call into Clive Burgess's corner shop. This was a typical 1970's corner shop where products segregation didn't exist. Bread was next to sweets that were next to beer that was next to the fire wood. From there it was down the hill heading towards Mount Pleasant Hospital and further down under the arched walk way of the old Technical College. Mount Pleasant hill was our gateway to the world. At the bottom was <u>Dynevor Comprehensive</u> for the first 3 years it was an all boys school where personally I did well. Then in the fourth year due to the old girls school at Lyn yr Bryn being utilized by Swansea College, girls were allowed into Dynevor. It's at this point my education started and it had nothing to do with math's!

A Phoenix over Llantwit Fadre

Swansea Clouds

Oh Swansea how I miss you
The beach, the parks and the sea
I remember all the holidays...
Running so wild and free.

Walking over the mountains
That took us to the world
Playing all our adventure games
Whilst the Dragons tail un-curled.

Running down the Black road
Would always end in pain
As we always ended up fighting
The North hill boy's again.

'Clive's' shop was on the corner
Just before the Farmers pub
A cave of sweets and chocolate
Of newspapers, fags and grub.

All summer long we walked and walked
And kicked along a ball
And climbed the ruins of any house
Climbing over any wall

Ring stone round is in the park
Where druids sing their song
So there we sat in festivals
Watching the beauties all day long

So Swansea how I miss you
My memories as a child
Playing cowboys and Indians
And riding rapids wild

Life was good in Swansea
But we had so little money
Yet the rain that fell upon my face
Tasted as good as pure Welsh Honey

I love going back to my home town
Swansea down by the sea
I hope one day to die there
That's where my soul can be.

I don't believe in the afterlife
Or Gods or Heaven's Gate
I just believe in Swansea
To be home I just can't wait

Severn Bridge, Beachley

Part 4

Like every child entering Swansea Market was like entering Aladdin's cave. The entrance on Oxford Street took you in... past the revolving stall. Of course, Health and Safety stopped it working many moons ago, the smells in the air would hit your nostrils immediately painting pictures in your mind of fresh bread, flower sellers and above all the pungent aroma of raw meat and fish. As a small kid walking past the fresh fish stalls was oddly exciting. To see the Hake with its mouth wide open showing razor sharp teeth, covered in ice and surrounded by a fan of Gamba's was the closest we got to deep sea exploring. There was a Welsh cake stall and an umbrella stall and best of all there were a couple of toy stalls. Nothing cost more than a pound but still too expensive for me, but still, to stand there holding my Mams hand I couldn't help but plan exactly what Father Christmas was going to bring me.

As a fifteen-year-old my first ever job was in the market on a stall selling burgers and chips on one side and ice cream on the other. Every Saturday and school holidays at last giving me a little money in my pocket. There was fresh fruit and veg, and of course cockles and laver bread and best of all Mrs. Jones selling flowers to whom everyone was a friend, everyone was her Cariad.

Priorities have changed so much during the pandemic, work, family, entertainment are all things we worry about, complain about and blame the Government for ruining. The one group of people however that just 'get on with it' are the brilliant medical teams in our NHS. These people go to work and then have to dress in Cylon Warrior armour in order to do their jobs. The heavy, uncomfortable and extremely hot PPE they have to wear just to save our lives, yet they don't complain, they don't threaten strikes and ask for pay rises or demand better latte flavours in the café, nurses just do it because they believe people are more important than any Politian's agenda or motive. When my Mam was dying the nurses would come in day after day with a smile, a reassuring look and just a simple hand on my shoulder and it meant so much. Who knows what sort of life they had back home. When Mam actually died the nurse who sat with me was I'm guessing close to finishing work to have a baby she was obviously close. Yet she sat uncomfortably on the little chair next to me and explained in a calm and clear voice exactly what would happen next and what I needed to do. She then helped me remove Mam's jewellery and her watch and went to get me a cup of coffee. Heavily pregnant but I was her priority.

The NHS

I woke up crying again it's the day after you died
I'm looking out of the window
How can people just carry on?
Don't they realize for their safety you are gone?...

Together we complained about the hours you worked
Together we complained about the money
But still I'd rather you be here tonight
Your scent as sweet as honey

But still those people are going to the park
Still they are going to the beech
Why can't they see it's their fault you died
Every idiot is still within its reach

I see them wearing a surgical mask
I'm sure they all think it's a movie
Walking around still within groups
Thinking ignorance makes them groovy

Why can't you come home tonight?
Why did you have to give your life
Trying to help those who chose to ignore
Who's mockery was as sharp as a knife

I woke up wanting to cry again,
it's a week now after you died
But I've decided the impotence of ignorant people
Won't diminish for you our pride

I now look out of the window
I don't care anymore about stupidity and shame to excess
For as a man, as a father, as a husband and for you
I am proud of the brilliant NHS.

The Knapp, Barry Island

Part 5

Our 2 bedrooms flat on Byron Crescent was our early home. The front door was strictly off limits especially on a Tuesday when the rent man was around. We were neither allowed near the windows to the front overlooking Waun Wen and Morfa beyond just in case the rent man saw us. The back door opened onto our veranda which housed our outside toilet and our coal bunker. Then down a couple of steps to the back gardens that without boundaries all merged into one. We played hide and seek, we did daring stunts on our make believe motor bikes and if the older boys were around we played War! The older boys were always the British and us young Uns were Germans. We always lost usually by one of us running in to our Mam because we had been punched or kicked or both. Just below the street was the Boys Club and below that The Rocks. Do gooders and Health and Safety nuts these days would have a heart attack if they saw us 6-7-year old's climbing over the rocks that became our battleship, our look out over Colburn and best of all the Star Trek Enterprise. We had the Bridge, the Engine room and even the lift all carved into the rock face.

 As always though we knew what not to do and especially we knew we had to be home by the time Mam had made tea. We were Mayhill kids, there was no such thing as lunch. It was breakfast, dinner and tea. Sometimes I feel sorry for kids today we had the world, today they have a controller.

   As youngster I sprouted up quickly so was one of the tallest, then when we hit around 15 years old I stopped growing when everyone else started and I was left behind.

The New Kid

There's a new kid on the block
His name is Covid-19
He knows everything about your life...
He knows everywhere you've been

With the promise of fun and gold and life
He will beckon you through the door
Then just as soon as he gets his way
He will make you a carrying whore

So when this evil child of men
Invites you out to play
Close the windows and the doors
Sit and sing not pray

For it is only men with bottles and plans
That gave life to Covid-19
Can you really say you aren't afraid
By the terrible news we have seen?

So please go and shop if you need to shop
Go to work if you must
Stop thinking we are all on holiday
Are these words too hard to trust?

Our people are dying all alone
No family or preacher to bless
Please let's start to be grown ups
Stay indoors, Save Lives and be human for once

And above all, praise our brilliant NHS
The NHS is not a fancy name for nurses and doctors to play
The NHS is the only way that we will survive this day
The NHS are not robots and fake people, they are humans like me and you
The NHS are risking their lives for the stupidity mankind can do
The NHS are my friends and yours, they are loved ones and family
So please for them, for yourself and your children stay at home so they too can be free
Coved-19 won't beat us
We can put up with the Boredom and stress
So again I will say, no I will bloody well shout!
Stay home and above everything-else, say thank you to the brilliant.

N-H -S!

Part 6

<u>Dynevor Comprehensive</u> was an inner-city school with very little facilities but passion in abundance. Truth be told we had a varied collection of teachers. My favourite was Mr. Craven our sports teacher, he was one of our sports teachers and one as kids we could have a real laugh with. We had reeking Rita, Spitfire Thomas, Tit-less Thomas, Ayatollah Thomas and scariest of all our Art teacher Sasquatch. Of course, these were all nice hard-working teachers but to us kids they were all the enemy. The school yard was our playground, teacher's car park and for my group of friends where we played handball. <u>Carl Dawkins</u> was the best and of course he was very shy about telling everybody. We had a school nurse whose cure for everything was a mouthful of milk of magnesia. Into building one there was 2 gym halls on top of each other, next 2 buildings classic class rooms. One of which was computer studies which I was banned from. The dinner canteen was a large room with a serving hatch at one end, we always went in last so we could have leftovers for free. Being a kid of a single parent, I received dinner tickets worth 55p which I usually sold for 60 or 70p each. The school was the second one to take the name of Dynevor first of which was attended by the great Welsh poet Dylan Thomas. Safe to say perhaps not much education was absorbed by me personally in school but thanks to my friends and a group of great teachers all with huge personalities I certainly learned loads.

Criccieth

    There were many girls who at some point in my early years caught my eye. However, there was one girl in school, who I won't name, just didn't see me. Through Juniors we were close friends, into <u>Dynevor Comprehensive</u> the girls went their own way to the girls school and even though on occasions we would meet the local girls to walk home from both schools respectively again she was never interested in me. We would usually meet them ...in the St. James area near Ffynone Drive. St. James Church was for a couple of us a Thursday evening get together. Supposedly it was to play Badminton but for myself and <u>Martin Heywood</u> it was a place to mess about, play Badminton and of course flirt. Gary Jones soon joined us and we would really enjoy our Thursday night out. In the final year of school, I broke the law and got myself a girlfriend from a rival school, Bishop Gore. A school in one of the more affluent area of Swansea and a school were education really mattered. All of a sudden, I was spending every spare moment in the Brynmill area. As I said earlier that was the difference between us then and my daughter's generation now. From Mayhill I walked to and from school, had food then walked from Mayhill to Brynmill and walked home again as long as I was home by 9.30pm. My route was varied either via Penlan Terrace, Ffynone Drive and the Uplands or sometimes down Constitutional Hill, officially one of the steepest roads in the world. Martin Henwood lived at the bottom and many times we would be seen runners up the hill as if filled with some invisible fuel.

Now I would probably struggle walking down. But this was Swansea it wasn't meant to be easy, to be comfortable and to ignore the beauty around us. It was ours to explore!

Working from home has put a whole new view on the role I have to do. Usually I would be driving the length and breadth of Wales visiting Stores, corner shops and your larger named brands such as Nisa, Budgens and Premier to name a few in order to sell our brand of Food To Go products and hopefully add some value and profit to their business. As we are owned by Brakes the supply chain has opened all lines so we can support our customers with any stock they may need not just our usual products.
The "F" word is dreaded every phone call made or taken.
Of course this "F" word is Flour!
I am not a particularly good sleeper so I write most of these bits and pieces in bed. My memory and my creative juices seem to work better with very little energy and just a hint of madness.

An evening view of Snowdonia

Part 7

Like all good circle of friends very few of us were known by our names. I was hairy so I was called Ape-man. We had Hunto and Spud, Lancey and The Head, we had froggy, whitey, snowy and Smutto. Names just meant different things. We called <u>Martin Henwood</u> Guinness because he dyed the front of his jet black hair white. We had Big bird and sprout, nelly and marshy and as for <u>Chris McDonald</u> there was no nicknames we all just felt sorry for him because he supported West Brom. We had a boy join us half way through called, James Norman Benedict Angus. He was something of a child protégé doing A level maths when he was 12 and adept at most instruments. Of course, there were others I've forgotten but we were a band of disjointed brothers. We also had races of all different backgrounds. Jaffrel Choudhry was a good friend and of course we all fondly remember Sukie. Sukwinder Singh was from a Sikh family. His Dad was actually an Elvis impersonator calling himself The Swinging Sikh. Sukie was a small ball of mischief. He was always winding up teachers, playing the fool and getting us all detention on a regular basis. Yet he was our friend, one of us.

I remember sitting in R.E. When after receiving a message the teacher Mr. Thomas told us, very sadly Sukie at the age of 13 years old had died overnight. For me and I assume many it was my first experience with death. The next couple of days were a blur in school and pretty soon we had been given details of the family's funeral arrangements. The school were supportive even laying on buses to take Sukies classmates and extended year friends to the funeral in Morriston Crem. The day arrived and one by one we were led single file passed the open coffin to pay our respects, it was the first dead body many of us had seen and for many it was just all too much. The following weeks were difficult. But as friends do, with jokes, with memories and of course the odd fight we got through. Especially us boys and girls from the Hill, we didn't have money, we didn't have big fancy houses, but those who had a Dad at home had respect. <u>Carl Dawkins</u> Dad was a giant with an even bigger heart, brilliant man. <u>David Harris</u> Dad took me and David to see the mighty Swansea City at the Vetch field for my first ever live game. Then there was our Mams. My mother even though very religious did enjoy a laugh and a joke, one of her best friends was Vera, Carl's Mam. I had more respect for Vera than any of my mother's sisters. <u>David Harris</u> Mam Was my mates Mam and clearly his friend and more of an Auntie to me again than any of my actual relatives. Mayhill born, Mayhill bread, strong in arm and .... no definitely not thick, proud!

Mousie Cutts

My Dad, Keith Aleman was one of the best story tellers I ever had the privilege to share a bottle or two of Dornfelter German Wine. As I didn't meet him until my early teens I never realised the influence he had on the way my Mam would entertain and teach us as little kids.

When the three of us were together, Mam, me and my brother Yan and as very young children when Mam wanted to get our attention she could quite literally morph her appearance into the character Mousie Cutts. Of course as it was for all intense purposes a cartoon like character alive and in front of us, we listened and reacted with excited and verve.

Mousie Cutts was a young female mouse who was very, very naughty. She was always getting into trouble for not speaking, or spelling properly and for getting into naughty adventures, such as writing on the bedroom walls. Her two naughty accomplices were Fido the dog, my brother Yan, and Baby who of course was me. To give an example Mousie would argue that there was sand in a dessert and you could eat a desert. It was Mams way of getting us to recognise words that sounded very similar, the similar spelling and of course how that word fits into a conversation. We could sit for hours laughing and playing and of course as us kids got tired we got irritable and so Mousie would start winding us up. Mam knew when it was time for Mousie to go to bed.

I mentioned my Dad's influence earlier. He was as I said a great story teller, he was also a great artist and cartoonist. One of his best characters was a young male mouse called Cherry Muffin who, as you guessed it, was a naughty mouse who used to get up to all sorts of adventures. Cherry Muffin had a number of companions, Jean-Paul the fat, alcoholic and not very bright French Mouse, there was Florinda, Cherry Muffins girlfriend and the Wizard. A remarkable mouse who was a Professor, a Teacher and a Wizard of which out of all three he was master of none!

The humour was dry and very innocent, the story telling imaginative and for kids exciting and just a little different. Also as an artist he wrote the stories and completed all of the cartoons to go with them himself. Just simple pen and ink drawings with minimal colour, enough only to emphasise what needed.

Even though they were only married for five years the roughly ten years they were together left so much influence of me Dads imagination on my mother.

Langorse Lake

Part 8

    Outdoor life was most definitely part of everything we did as kids. There were versions of gaming machines and even versions of personal computers but nothing like today's technology. No for us every second not n school and not watching our Black and White TV which took 50p coins to use, was spent outside. Personally, I enjoyed the A team and Starsky and Hutch, but my favorite program was about a Chinese not very bright "God" called Monkey. It was the story of four companions travelling across medieval China and having adventures along the way. But apart from TV and no matter what the weather was we were out. Walking around Nicander Parade we had brilliant views of Swansea Bay and before I ever went there I used to love sitting on one of the benches overlooking Swansea, especially on football days when Swansea City were playing at home as I could see the Vetch Field and even though I couldn't see the actual pitch or play I could imagine and picture exactly what was happening just by the sounds being made by the supporters luckily enough to be there. Then later in the day back on the Green we would all re-Enact everything we had heard. The only live football back then on TV was a cup final. We had 3 channels and half the programs were in Welsh. There was not very much to complicate life, you watched what was on or you went out to play. Of course after watching the 1980 FA Cup Final between Arsenal and West Ham United, after Alan Devonshire crossed for Trevor Brooking to head the only and winning goal of the match I fell in love with West Ham United. Apart from my beloved Swansea City, West Ham would most certainly be my second following. **Life was simple** get up, go to school, come home, play football and repeat.

Out of Reach

Walking past the window I look and see the world
The world is different now
There is a poison in the air and it's bringing death
The world is different and how?

There's a man who cries whilst waiting for a bus
The world is painful tonight
There is no friend to keep him safe
The world seems to have forgotten the fight.

There is a pain that grows in every Dad
The world is slow to give
Tonight every mother wishes and prays
The world can't simply let us live

There are people dressed in green and blue
Their world is a painful mess
Yet they sacrifice their own
Because you can't live with stress

The world outside this window
The world is full of sorrow
And if only you could keep Out of reach
Our NHS heroes will have a tomorrow

Byron Crescent was matched in famous names by Lord Byron's poetry peer, Lord Shelley. Just below the front entrances to Byron Crescent was and, on the corner, Iris Gowes shop. If you can imagine a house which had been blackened by a house fire then you can picture the inside decoration of the shop. It was black, no lights of any substance, no fridges and no hygiene of any kind. I suppose because of the time, early- mid seventies, hygiene and cleanliness perhaps weren't as prevalent as they are now. Fresh milk was kept under the counter, no fridge. I can remember going in to buy a balloon and Iris would insist in a strange customer care-ish way of blowing it up first. Yuk! As a 6-7-year-old I can remember being sent to the shop by my mother for ten Bensons 37p I think they were. Just passed was the Swansea Boys Club. An exposing building back then. The boys club started as the Strand Mission in 1922 and at one point was one of the most successful football-oriented clubs in Wales. The Strand Mission was a religion led organization who wanted to do something for young boys who had finished school but had nothing to do outside of work. Local police acknowledged that youths having nothing to do could cause trouble so therefore supported the club. The original building was in the city centre and very soon by offering P.E. Football, table tennis and swimming it very quickly took off. The club had a motto "Straight and True" and at the start of every session the boys had to say a pledge.

"I promise that with the help of God, I will endeavor to be honest, straightforward and manly in my daily life and I will do all I can to promote the interest of our club"

So, it is such a shame that over the years it has been ransacked, burgled and left to, well, fall to its proverbial knees. As kids we loved playing football in the main hall, or playing pool upstairs and then having a giggle whilst trying to look macho in the disco room. The building stands, a dirty pink eyesore overlooking the East side of Swansea. There is still much speculation about what can or what will happen but as someone who spent enjoying all sorts of shenanigans in there, I think it's really quite sad.

Part 9

     Most of our Mams I'm guessing were born around the time of World War 2. Times were hard. We are all fed up right now at having to stay at home but still we have all of the luxury our own homes offer. My mother Pauline was born in 1941 on Cwm Farm which was in the valley just below Cefn Coed Hospital. The 3-story farm house had electricity only on the ground floor which was the kitchen and the living room all in one. There were a couple of steps up to the middle room which was for best and upstairs were the two bedrooms. There was no running water. The toilet was outside and for water it was a hundred-yard walk to the stream. Cwm Farm was rented off the Council by Thomas Ellis my Grandfather. He had no skill or interest in farming so he sublet the two fields to other farmers as a place to keep their animals. As kids and indeed with some school friends we loved playing up in the forest area called the Graig. I remember David Harris being taken Ill once in my Aunts house now owners of the farm and throwing up in her living room. My mother's old house by now was a stable and Pauline Aleman as she was now couldn't bear to go near it. The entrance to the farm was just off the road by the Cockett Inn. It was a walk down a dirt track with large metal gates which got their name from the fact they were only ever opened for funerals. The Funeral Gates had a small gate to one side for people to walk through. But it was a steep, muddy and quite isolated track. My mother's upset was due to her Father and Brothers behaviour towards my Grandma, her mother Alice. I was born years after her death but many people told me Alice was one of the nicest people you could meet. Post war Swansea there was very little work, many people were mourning lost loved ones and money was scarce. Thomas and my Uncle Armyne always found money to visit the Cockett Inn and would regularly return home in the early hours drunk and for whatever reason set upon my Grandma Alice often beating her for no reason. As the youngest and only child still at home, her brothers and sisters were all much older, she recounts walking up the track in the middle of the night, in the pitch black, whatever the weather and usually bare foot to find help on the main road. There were no phones, no way to communicate other than finding someone, anyone who could fetch the police. By the time she got back home the men were sleeping off the drink and temper and Grandma would be forgiven them and blaming herself. This was my Mams life as a kid. After going to school in Townhill and finishing her school years in Gore Avenues School she started working in Smiths Crisps factory in Fforestfach.

The farm is now privately owned and on the site of the old house is a Mediterranean style Villa and there are now houses built on the fields. I know my mother's sister-in-law lived there until the mid 1990's, for how long after I don't know.

We mock when older people say things like "You don't know how lucky you are these days ". Being close to the older generation now it's only now we can see how hard our parents, especially our Mams had life as they grew up. We as kids hard it hard compared to our kids these days but back then it must have been terrible. Yes, there was love, there was caring and indeed good times also, but everyday life must have been a struggle, every day.

Living through this Coronavirus pandemic we are all thinking how difficult life is. Nando's where my daughter works is shut so as a 19 years old she is stuck in the house with me apart from shopping or walks. Her I-phone is on for her music and her various viewing channels such as Netflix are fully utilized. Kid's are bored, fed up and wishing they were back at school just saw they can spend time with their mates. Even though there is stupidity going on with panic buying there is no shortage realistically of food and even though stuck at home we, none of us have got it hard. Yes I know there are many people with varying and different personal problems but generally we are ok.

Most of our parents were born during or just after World War 2. They grew up either knowing or knowing of a loved one, friend or neighbour who lost their lives either abroad on the battlefield or at home with the Blitzkreig. They grew up without the internet, mobile phones and the latest Nike trainers. Money was scares and of course food was still rationed for some time. Yet they got through life and lived so that obviously we could arrive. I would imagine for many of our parents no matter how house proud our Grandparents were the conditions they were brought up would horrify many of our kids today. Outside toilets? No TV? And God forbid…no wi-fi?

Langorse Lake

  Both Byron Crescent and Shelley Crescent it could be said had dubious characters. Living next door to us was Stan, I never knew his surname or really anything about who and where he is from. What we did know is that he would walk the streets collecting scrap and broken wood. He would bring it home and after drying it out he would chop it into small bundles of firewood. He would then again walk the streets this time selling the bundles to neighbours and surrounding streets at 5p a go. When not chopping wood he would stand out on his veranda and with a woodbine cigarette gripped firmly by yellow stained fingers he would watch the world go by. His dark grey shirt I imagine was once a brilliant white and the waffle tank top he wore on top of it had more holes than Donald Trump's hairstyle. If whatever reason we got inside his flat, usually for a lend of money for Mam, the flat just oozed blackness. No colour, no pictures, no electric lighting just dirt and soot marks left by the ever burning coal fire that also doubled as his cooker and oven. Stan had short spikey black hair that was slowly turning an odd greyish yellow on the edges was challenged for prominence by the caterpillar eyebrow that sat across the whole of his forehead and stood guard over sad and lonely eyes. The bristles on his chin were starting to give defensive grey hairs on a once clean shaven face and for now his appearance was of no concern, to anyone.

Stan's heart was pure, his motives were all about helping. The friendship us little kids had with him would be frowned upon today but back then we all thought this strange, enigmatic old man was a legend.'

Langorse Lakes

A story of the Pain

His whole body can tell a story
Of betrayal, of love and of war
Where money shouts the loudest
And holy men love the price of a whore

There is no scar or bruise left
To remember all his pain
And no matter what the leaders say
Children will be killed again

Mankind has turned from God and prayers
Mankind has become a bore
For everyone thinks they the right
To buy themselves a war

Yet in these times of debt and pain
With people still risking their lives
The selfish children of mankind
Are killing husbands and wives

You don't need a machete in your hand
There is no upper hand to gain
By ignoring the rules of Covid-19
You are writing the story of Pain

Please don't be fooled by the famous and rich
Their bubbles are thick with posh glass
They can carry on in the world they can afford
You must just sit on your arse.

Don't be envious or greedy or angry at God
Crying to him will just fall on deaf ears
The holy men have been asking him why?
He's been ignoring mankind for years

Look after yourself and all of your clan
Don't bask in the idiot's glory
Stay at home, protect the NHS
Let's take pain out of our story!

Part 10

    A similar chap was Willy Crowley. If anyone was ever a spy, a serial killer or any sort of wanted outlaw from a previous life it was him. Nobody appeared to know anything about him other the pungent odour that seemed to follow him everywhere he went. None of us kids would dare go near the steps taking down to his flat's back door. If a ball ever happens to get kicked or thrown down it was like a football team of Ninjas creeping down to get them. The gap just before his back door welcomed you as if you about to go cave diving. It was cold, dark and smelly. Close by were my mother's friends Pat with her 5 kids, and Megan whose kids were Debbie, Jackie and sadly missed brother David. Pat and Megan as far as I was concerned were family. There was John Henry who kept horses in the back garden, no fence just a rope tied to a spike in the ground to keep the house close. Once a month us little kids would follow him around the back gardens as he would hunt and shoot rats with his gun. Health and Safety?

There was Dillys opposite us on Shelley Crescent with her husband Eric and their son David was another few door down from them. The other side to Dillys was iris Gowe and her husband Ken. David Harris lived the other end of Byron Crescent with Paul Leonard further over on Waun Wen hill.

Our two bedrooms flat had the bath in the kitchen, an outside toilet and a coal fire for hot water in the living room. All these years later, 44 years or so have passed, I remember it so vividly. Especially the bright horrific Sun Flower wallpaper my mother insisted on having.

Swansea from Nicander Parade

So once again I can't sleep, usually it's because of the medication I take for lovely bits of metal holding my back together, and yes, I really do have a screw loose. It's floating near the sciatic nerve, so they won't touch it. No tonight, or this morning, I can't sleep because the isolation now adventurers back then thingy I am writing with all my brilliant friends from school has got me thinking of the situation we all find ourselves in and the people who matter now and those who are no longer here. If my son Kristofer was alive, he would be 28 in September. So much hope for a glorious future just...gone! My Mam would be 79 in December. With Yan and my sisters Helene and Rhiannon in Germany life could be incredibly lonely. Luckily though my beautiful daughter Olivia is in isolation with me and my girlfriend, my best friend Jo is just around the corner. Not being able have a cwtch is horrible but at least when I'm walking the dogs I can call to Jo's home and chat even if from a distance. I feel terrible for Olivia she is 19 in two weeks and her birthday will be at home with me not being able to see her mother. I know she FaceTime's her, but everyone needs Mam now and again. Hopefully by the time this is all over Olivia will have found out what Fairy washing up liquid is used for. Our dogs Lola and Boo love their daily walk I only wish I could take them out more. Since moving from Brecon where they were out 4 or 5 times a day, I have neglected them somewhat.

To all my friends from Swansea I say thank you, I haven't seen you for over 30 years yet here we are talking as if we see each other every day. The last time I saw anyone was when Paul Leonard came to my mother's funeral. Please keep the stories going and please add to anything I write; this whole experience is breath-taking. I'm going to try and keep these going through all these scary times and who knows perhaps even put it all into a book for us all. I'm honoured you are my friends and yes, we must all meet up after this if Desmond William Hughes doesn't organise it. Take Care my friends, let's keep the stories going. My love to you all.

I'm adding this bit probably 3 or 4 months after writing the portion above, we still haven't been able to have our school reunion and sadly thanks to recent events it doesn't look as if it will happen anytime soon. I live in the county of Rhondda Cynon Taff which has just been put back into lock-down. I have been having treatment for the nerve damage in my spine and shoulder which is affecting my left arm and even though that doesn't stop me from doing anything the constant pain is dragging me down. I am already being treated for severe depression via medication and just taking the extra pain relief I have been prescribed is so restricting. I feel constantly tired because I can't sleep, I'm not eating properly and working mainly from home is not ideal so again is restricting what I can do. I'm just fed up. Both my daughter and my girlfriend are putting up with my moods.

In school you have friends and best friends and people who are literally like family. You have connections with different people at different times for different reasons. Paul Davies, Mark Hunt and I for example loved football. Stu Oakley and I had a similar passion in music, Nik Kershaw, Paul Hardcastle for example. With Martin Henwood it was just flirting with every female we could. Martin was also football mad and he was a ball boy for the mighty Swans. David Harris was the intelligent one of us and Paul Leonard the most athletic. Carl Dawkins again loved football but he just stood in front of the goalie waiting for the ball to come to him. Ha-ha.

Dynevor Comprehensive had two gyms. The lower floor was for climbing frames, horse boxes and so on whilst the top floor was for football and basketball especially. We were a motley Crewe of boys we either preferred sport or education there was no one who seemed to fit in both categories. Mr. Brian Jones took rugby alongside Mr. Howell who alongside Ray Craven took us in football. They were all rugby oriented people so tackling waste height in football was accepted especially by Michael Wheeler. Chopper Wheeler was undoubtedly the best footballer we had in our ranks. Obviously, kit mattered and getting me kit was not something my mother prioritised. I wore £5 football boots with plastic studs from Woolworths, I had worn them so much they had no tongue in them and studs were almost flat. The only form of kit I had were tracksuits my brother no longer used from the Army. The only real bit of kit I had were my goalie gloves. I remember on one occasion Mr. Craven was winding us up so we all, young kids, piled him. It was great fun and fair play he joined in with the humour it deserved. When girls arrived in Dynevor it was a different world. All of a sudden, the little girls we were in junior school with were stood in front of us with boobs and figures. On a sad note my big crush was Julie Minister but she was only interested in an education. School was great and terrible, fun and miserable but most of all it was a learning experience however wrong that experience was.

My daughter Olivia was born April 24th, 2001. Every other Sunday for the next couple of years I took her to Swansea to spend time with my Mam. As Olivia grew older the bond grew stronger and stronger. As Mam lived in a red bricked house on Creidiol Rd, Olivia called her Nanny Red House.
Roughly at the start of April 2005 my mother's friend phoned me to say he was worried as he couldn't get an answer at Mams house. I drove the forty-five miles only to find her and Ronald having a cuppa. Yes, she was tired and ashen but otherwise the same. In between Christmas and New Year 2004 and at the time of the Tsunami that killed so many in Indonesia, Mam was told that she had lung cancer. It was pea size in her left lung just above the valve for the heart. The doctor explained it wasn't going to kill her as it was too small but because of where it was it would hamper her breathing. 51 years of smoking didn't help. Over the next few months as long as she had her coffee, the odd cheese sandwich and her fags, which she hid from Ronald, she was happy. Olivia's birthday was 6 weeks away and on our usual visit we walked around the green and over to the edge of Nicander Parade to look out over Swansea. It was the beginnings and of March but it was beautiful weather, it was warm and sunny, perfect. After that Mams health just went downhill, it was if she had given up. just as before Ronald phoned me on a Friday night to say he was worried as once again Mam wasn't answering the door, by the time I had reached Mam phoned to say she had simply fallen asleep, I turned around. The next morning whilst at the gym I had 4 missed calls from Ronald. I drove straight down and Mam was sitting on the sofa and her skin was white. I called an ambulance and within minutes we were all sat in Singleton Hospital. After tests and a couple of hours on an oxygen mask doctors came by and said Mams oxygen level was low so they were going to keep her in for a couple of days and then she should be fit to go home. That was Saturday afternoon. By Tuesday she had fallen into a coma. The next couple of weeks were a blur, work was brilliant and supported everything I needed to do. I was getting up, going to Swansea, going home and repeat the next day. Olivia's 4th birthday party came

and went. Then a week after on May 1st I had to just go home and sleep. Mam was very religious as many of you know and even though I respected her views I was and still am a firm atheist. Members of her church would come into her room and sit there praying, I hated it. As it was the end of the football season and there was a lot of football on TV, I made sure it was always on and turned up full. I slept downstairs and at 12:20am on May 2nd I was phoned by the hospital to come down. The drive to Swansea alone, not knowing exactly what I was going to find and obviously scared was horrific. An hour later I got into her room to be told Mam had passed away. The fear left me and looking at Mam she looked beautiful, peaceful and pain free. The lovely nurse in her room must have been 8 months or more pregnant, I felt bad that she was having to deal with me. I removed Mams, rings, her watch and then kissed on her on the forehead. I told her I loved her and promised her Olivia would always know all about her. The drive home was a blur I spent the next hour driving and phoning those that needed to know. It was a Bank Holiday so everything had to wait for a day. Emptying her house was a task and a half. There were bags of sugar, jars of coffee and other goods piled high as if she just the same shop every week regardless to need. The Council only give me the week to empty the house or they were going to charge me rent, work gave me a van to use and Ronald and a couple of Mams other friends all mucked in. We got it done. In two weeks, it will be 15 years, May 2nd, what makes it harder is that my son Kristofer died on May 3rd, different years but still, I hate the beginning of May

Aberystwyth

Part 12

1977 saw the opening of the Leisure Centre in Swansea. I can remember waiting for hours in the blazing sun as Army and RAF cadets lined the roads leading to the new building waiting for the Queen to arrive to open it. You could see one by one as cadets fainted from the excitement and heat of the day. The royal cavalcade eventually zoomed past and the anticlimax was complete. However, it did mean a group of us would go swimming on a I think a Monday evening. There was an amazing invention called a wave machine which as it sounds created waves and a spring board into the deepest pool you had ever seen. Upstairs there was a skittle alley and two pool tables. For a teenager in 1980s Swansea it was heaven. If we had enough money we would stop in the KFC on High St before catching the number 11 bus back home. The bus would stop outside Eagen Chip Shop and down Townhill Road to the shops where Carl Dawkins, Julie Minister and Jayne Rowe would get off. A couple of others used to come as well but I can't remember who? Swimming has always been a big thing for me, I love water. For the time I worked in Egypt being in the pool was a necessary way of relaxing. In the hotel I worked we had the largest freshwater pool in Egypt. Egypt was an experience to behold. If we ever wanted to go to another town, I worked on Elphantine Island near the Aswan Dam, we would need to book the police to escort us two weeks in advance. I asked once why there is no glass in the windows of the buses and trains thinking it was to do with the heat, only to be told if locals know there are Americans on board they would openly shoot. So, with no glass if you don't get shot then hopefully you won't get hurt by flying glass. One of my duties was to teach golf to the hotel guests in the afternoon. I asked one day what is the clicking noise I can hear when near the Nile thinking, frogs, insects. No, I was told it was Crocodiles clicking their teeth telling us to stay away. I remember, quite surprising that Osama Bin Ladin was a hero to many. Of course, we didn't know back then about the terror intended by Al Qaeda, but it was everywhere. Our guide when first arriving told us always to barter with market stall holders, I tried once to buy a caftan priced at 30 Egyptian pounds , about £5, I offered 15 Egyptian pounds and he took out a huge dagger put it to his own throat until he drew blood and explained I might as well kill him by wanting to pay less money. I paid the full price. I met up with a lady whose husband was an airline pilot. She visited Egypt regularly and would buy a cheap Walkman to use whilst there. The waiter or waitress or staff member of the hotel who looked after her the best she would give the Walkman knowing they would sell it for enough money to feed their family for 2-3 months. I liked Egypt. Felt like home.

Llyn Tecwyn Uchaf

Part 13

Growing up on a Council Estate in 1970's Swansea there was no choice on whether we went out to play, we were out all weathers. When it snowed it really snowed? I can remember sitting on black bin bags at the top but if the Black Road and sliding down without a care in the world. I slid down one time ripping both my trousers and pants and grazing the whole of my right-hand arse cheek. We never had gloves if it was that bad, we couldn't go without we would wear socks on our hands. It was very rare for school to be shut so very often we would spend the day in school with soaking wet clothes. Then the walk home all uphill would be cold, uncomfortable and exhausting. Admittedly my attendance was probably average in the last couple of years, not like Carl Dawkins who I think never missed a day. School was the only interaction we had for most of the winter and so during bad weather we enjoyed actually being there. There was no central heating or tumble dryer so as soon as I got home, I would have to strip and hang my clothes in the airing cupboard. The coal fire would be roaring with enough coal in the bucket for the night ahead. As there was only heat in the living room going upstairs to listen to music or actually going to bed would mean practically getting fully dressed all over again. We had a 2-bar electric fire and if any of my mates came round to listen to my record collection Mam would let me put the fire on, one bar for one hour. It's funny we always say things like "kids today have got it easy ". But it's true. The best thing though was we were all a family. If I was in David Harris house near dinner time his Mam would make me dinner. I can also remember Vera, Carl Dawkins Mam sitting me in front of the fire until I was warm. All our Mams cared for all of us. We were all a family. After moving away to work, to London, Egypt and moving away from Swansea to get married I lost touch with everyone. Then out of the blue after I had left my wife Carl Dawkins contacted me on Facebook and the gates were opened. So, to be back in touch with all of my friends from school I have to say thank you to Carl.

Aberystwyth

Sunday's as a kid was always a strange day. For a while every Sunday a group of us would go to Cwmdonkin Park. I remember Chris McDonald, Lynda Joyce, Jayne Rowe, Julie Minister, Carl Dawkins and David Harris for a few. We would play on the swings and climbing frames and at the top of the park amongst the trees we would plat hide and seek. Tim Rickard was one of my mates at the time but as his Dad was a Pastor in Church, Tim wasn't allowed out on Sundays. Cwmdonkin Park was a good 4-5 miles from most of our homes yet there was no worry or concern, as long as we were home at a reasonable time. David Harris and I went through so much as friends, fights, being bullied, laughing and most of all playing together. If one person in my life as a kid was and still is treasured its David. Thank you. No matter who we teamed up with we always ended up playing together. Mary, David's Mam, his Auntie Susie and indeed all his family were always welcoming, and above treated me as part of the family. Sunday was a strange day for me also, as a small child totally against my will every Sunday was my mother making us go to church. I hated it. I must say I must be one of the few atheists who can recite the bible.

Sitting in the uncomfortable wooden pews when it came to prayer time my brother would lean forward on the little shelf on the back of the pew in front, on one occasion fits of laughter were only hidden by the sound of his snoring as he had fallen asleep. The funniest time in church came later, when my Mam decided to be baptised wanting to get a better view, so Yan and I went upstairs to look down on the proceedings. As the pastor lowered my mother backwards into the water she obviously sucked in a large amount of water and having coughed and spluttered for breath ending up sending her false teeth suddenly floating across the water. As teenagers we just collapsed with laughter. Pretty soon going to church was a real no and so Sunday was another day to have fun. Swansea as a kid was fun. Fields, trees, parks and girls. So, it all began.

Saturday mornings as a kid in Swansea changed many times ove4vthe years depending on age and how much money we had. One favourite was going to the Odeon Cinema above Tesco on the Kingsway for Saturday morning club. It cost 50p to get in and it usually take the whole week to get the money together. The cinema would usually show a couple of cartoons, a hero type series like Zorro for example and a Movie, usually made by the British Film Foundation. Before and in between each show there was a psychedelic pink display on the giant screen and in the background the instrumental hits of the Shadows would be playing out loud. I do remember however a couple of times a band or solo artist playing on the stage in front of the screen. Other Saturday mornings were spent in Swansea Library, swimming in the Leisure Centre or if money wasn't a problem, if we had a fortune like a £1! Then it would be the Carousel Amusement Arcade underneath the Valbonne nightclub. We were 6 or 7 years old yet we were safe going into to town and our Mams knew we would be home on time. There was no drama or theatrics. Yes, I dare say all the bad things were around then but without 24/7 news and the internet we didn't see it, hear it or fear it. In the summer practically every family in the street would walk to the beech all excited, full of fun and joking around on the way and crying, whinging and little gits all the way home. You know we have always said about leaving doors open and neighbours just walking in and out, and it was true. All neighbours we family. Discipline was there too however. I can remember a friend's mother putting washing powder in his mouth for swearing, having a slap was normal if you were naughty. Again, no theatrics, it was normal. I don't think many of us have turned too bad, except Paul Leonard

One Book

There's a magic book which tells a man
 How to grow and stake a stance
 But will pages of books really speak
 And give mankind a chance?

Since the beginning of time a word is spoken
 A word of fire, of illusion and lust
 All these things lay in the heart
 And make mankind do as he must

So why is it now when time as past
 Mankind can't start again
 For nobody now can read a book
 Yet mankind welcomes pain

There are gardens and tablets and pyramids too
 There are men in robes who just tell
 There are people who buy lives everyday
 Not caring of the children, they sell

There is hurt and hate all over the world
 Right now, we are all in a mess
 But common sense is nowhere to be seen
 As people still threaten the great NHS

This virus, this hate, this loathing of life
 Has given us a reason to make a stance
 Stay indoors and read a book
 Please, give us all a chance.

Part 14

The walk from Mayhill to Swansea beach was a downhill walk and an uphill stress generator for our Mams. If all my Mams friends with all their kids went there could be 20+ in our strange caravan. The walk would always take us past the YMCA down St. Helens Rd, past the majestic Guildhall and Swimming baths, next after running past Victoria Park us kids would scream with excitement as we run up the steps of the old slip bridge. The bridge cradled Oystermouth Rd and gave impressive views of the coast Running down the other side without a care in the world we would jump into the powdered soft sand and scream again with joy. The whole shebang would set up camp on the beach usually near the arches under the bridge. It may be a false image but I'm sure at one point there were swings on the sand near the arches. Due to the location and tidal habits of Swansea the tide was only normally in early morning and tea-time, wrong times of the day for swimming but a perfect occasion for us to play in the Granny's Custard, look for crabs and just be free. Mam would have brought crisps and tip tops which by now were liquid but still nice and cold and so refreshing. There was no worry or knowledge of skin cancer so sun burn was a required badge from going to the beach. I remember once having blisters from sun burn on my back and one of the other kids jumping on my back inviting a scream and many tears from me. The sand was warm and like all kids we played football or chased each other and on the odd occasion we caught the tide in we had a great time jumping over waves, diving and generally having a brilliant time. Then the point came 5o start the long walk home. We were all shattered, hungry and by now miserably dreading the walk retracing our steps to include the Everest like climb, Mount Pleasant Hill. "Can we have chips, can we have a Jo's, can we have a drink and can we get a bus?" These questions were repeated by all the kids falling on deaf ears of all the Mams. The half our walk down would be a two hour walk home with us kids by now arguing and our Mams just longing to get us bathed and into bed and more importantly out of sight. Weather permitting, we would do it all again a week later.

It didn't matter if we were kids from single parents or had both Mam and Dad at home, times were hard and most of the time we were skint. I remember going to the Mr. Whippy Ice Cream van and asking him for any broken cornets for free. And as many people say about the past, we ate what was put in front of regardless what it was. Of course, sometimes food can be just as horrendous as starvation. I went to stay with my Dad in Berlin and his girlfriend decided to cook. Now my food heaven is chicken my food hell is mushrooms.

The day Dagmar decided to cook she stuffed a whole chicken with what appeared to be millions of mushrooms and then tied it shut and boiled the whole thing for hours, the flat stunk within minutes of this horrible smell, so much my Dad and I left and spent the rest of the day in a Turkish cafe bar. I can remember Mam just doing her best to make meals, it was usually something and chips. I can remember having tea at David Harris house one night and his Mam Mary made ham, beans and boiled potatoes, I thought I was in heaven. Nowadays I enjoy cooking and through a leisure company I worked for I'm trained to cook Singapore food, but my favourite is a Sunday dinner. Tomorrow is my daughter Olivia's 19 Birthday and so to celebrate, obviously we can't go out, we are having a Chinese delivered. Food has always played varied parts in our lives, when Kristofer died, I lost 4 stone, after I had surgery on my spine, I put it all back on. On one occasion however that haunts me about food I only remembered after my Mams funeral. I know we by now were in Creidiol Rd and I can remember walking home from school with Julie Minister and a couple of others when my Mam and brother met me half way to say we were going to the cinema. A truly magnificent story was being told of a young boy fight between good and evil...in a galaxy a long, long time ago. Star Wars was the film. Unknown to me Mam had saved for months, robbed Peter to pay Paul and somehow, we were going to see it. The walk down to the Odeon was full of fun and excitement, the film was breath taking and afterwards Mam even had enough money for the bus home. Then....the bus stopped outside Eagan Chip Shop and we wanted chips, but all Mams money was gone, did we care, shit no! All the way along Nicander Parade walking home we gave her grief. Mam had skimped and saved for who knows how long to take us to the cinemas and this is her thanks. I can picture her sitting on the sofa crying, I didn't remember any of this until after she died. A funny episode with food or should I say fruit, we went on a school trip to Manor Park in Tenby, on the way home David Harris pulls out a large, soft, bright red apple and still holding it falls asleep. Whilst he was asleep, we managed between us to eat the apple whilst David was still holding it so when he woke, he just had the core being held tightly in-between his fingers.

Today and I have to say for some time I have been a porridge junkie, I love the stuff. Jo my girlfriend has changed my eating habits, I was quite happy going without food for long lengths of time before, I like food, but I can do without also. Jo has taught me to look after myself better and I'm sure her beautiful Mam Pat thinks I'm wasting away, there is always something great to eat as soon as I walk in. One of the side effects of working for a food distribution company is that you get bored with food. How I long for a drunken Steak by Night.

Trwysffynydd

Going back a couple of hundred years my Dads family left SAN Heppolito in Mexico and for generations settled in Lalinia, Spain. After the Great War the whole of Europe was hit hard by unemployment and so Jose Aleman my Grand Father set to sea via merchants shipping to find fortune and soon ended up in the "Cuban" pub close to both the docks and Wind St in Swansea. This particular area of Swansea in the 1920s,1930s and beyond was well known for drinking dens, crimes of any and every description and of course Salubrious Passage where Ladies of a certain vocation could quite easily tempt sailors back from months at sea from both their dignity and their money. Wind St when we were growing up was the street for second hand shops, dodgy pubs and the first Argos in Wales opened there. Wind St was a favourite haunt of Dylan Thomas and for years for decent people to avoid. Of course, these days the life of Swansea has moved from the Kingsway where all Swansea night life used to be down to a much improved and vastly cleaner Wind St all together.

Many of the old banks and respected businesses are now pubs and even though its 15 years or so since I walked down it, and please correct me if I'm wrong, I think now it's pedestrianised apart from delivering trucks. The Terminus pub was one of the pubs my work mates and I would frequent every night playing pool, bogeying to the juke box or just necking in the corner by the fruit machine with whatever student had come to work with us for a few months. Being of a certain build and strength to match I was regularly the fight breaker upper, or peacekeeping force. My strength has always kept me in good stead. Even though I, like others was bullied in Junior school I've never been one for aggressive behaviour. I never believed in using my strength in anything other than sport. I remember Tim Rickard and I decided to "play" boxing in his perfectly square, just like a boxing ring, front garden. We both had boxing gloves on and giggling away threw punches with little effect at each other, then me being clever lowered my gloves and Tim just lunged at me knocking me out cold with a full punch to the chin. Perhaps not fully out cold but god, it felt like. Of course, as 11-12-year olds then it wasn't A&E it was cold flannel and a cup of tea to put things right. Swansea was a City now and the whole world seemed to be pouring in. In school Asian boys became good friends, we didn't care about skin colour, we had a couple of Chinese boys in another year, we just didn't care. No matter where in the world you came from if you could kick a football and support Swansea City you were a mate. These days apart from my daughter all my family alive are in Germany. Even my Great Uncle Harry the Hook in USA has been dead for many years. Harry Aleman was part of Chicago and SAN Francisco mafia. It was proved he murdered 12 people but he was accused of killing 98. With everything going on in the world today it's Olivia and my girlfriend Jo that keep me sane, well sort of.

I have two very dear friends Julie and Simon, and sometimes not having close family around me is great when I see family feuds going on and then sometimes, even as a 50+ year old all I want is to be wrapped in my Mams arms. Trying to tell kids these days how important your family is I think goes on deaf ears.

For weeks we have been under Lockdown. Covid-19 has taken over our lives. We are told it started in China around November last year and its only now a vaccine is being created. Undoubtedly there are conspiracy theories about Government created chemical weapons and I wouldn't be surprised to find out if ET was being blamed somewhere. All I know for sure that if my Mam was alive it would be a punishment from God, or a game with the devil. Prayers would be being said forgiveness, understanding and guidance would be begged for.
Many years ago, I had a wee Scottish lady as my boss. She was no more than four feet and a fart, but hell could be found behind every tooth let alone a bell.

This was at a time when being a short, middle aged angry Scottish lesbian was a massive hurdle for her to overcome every day, but she did, because everything was treated as simply and honestly as possible. One of her favourite sayings I still use today, "if something isn't right it doesn't mean it's wrong, it only becomes wrong if you don't attempt to put it right" in other words stop talking about Lockdown and tests and doing this and not doing that, just bloody find a cure! Is it that easy? Of course, if you follow the Orange President you just drink or inject bleach, but surely there are enough resources in the world to stop this. I remember when AIDs first hit the headlines, it was the end of the world, yet now people can live normal lives with medical help if they have AIDs. I think what I'm trying to say is that I believe world leaders don't have a priority regarding Coronavirus. Instead of Richard Branson asking for Government financial help, spend a bit of your own £4.8 Billion to pay your staff. Let that money from the government buy PPE for example. I get the impression every country wants to be the Super Hero for beating Coronavirus. Perhaps and only perhaps, if Every country worked as ONE on this, who knows, perhaps we can all be human beings again.

Hay on Wye

Do You Remember?

Do you remember bee's busily buzzing?
Do you remember birds singing in a tree?
Do you remember the promise you made once?
To keep our children free?

Do you remember the waves loudly crashing?
Do you remember dogs barking to save a friend?
Do you remember throwing away your ambition?
And welcoming to our world it's end?

Do you remember the government asking us to stay at home?
Do you remember telling loved ones, we can still talk on the phone?
Do you remember telling everyone it's going to be ok?
Then going on the piss last night coz you can have your way?

Do you remember being told the numbers of people who had died?
Do you remember how your brother felt, do you remember how he cried?
Do you remember how you felt listening to the Boris loving bores?
No, you forgot everything, and you wouldn't stay indoors.

I remember the countryside, the beautiful beach and more
I remember laughing and dancing through the door
I remember people, I remember how I cried
I remember Covid and the day the NHS died.

Aberystwyth

During this current pandemic I like so many are working from home. We are into the 8th week now and I hate it. It's the same routine day in day out. I usually get up 5:30am or there about and sit having my coffee watching the news and the dogs run in and out of the garden. My ex-wife used to call me a walking radiator, I enjoy the cold and love windows and doors to be wide open as much as possible. When the Council decided to refurbish the flats of Byron Crescent and we moved up to Creidiol Road it was just the same living conditions except we had stairs and an inside toilet. There was a coal fire in the living room and a coal fire in the kitchen. I think I can recall the kitchen one being used twice, certainly no more than three times. Just like Byron the coal fire was our only source of heating the water. For extreme cold and only if Mam had any money for the electric meter which took 50p pieces, we would be allowed to turn on the two bar electric fire that only had one bar working. We had a meter for the electric and a meter on the TV from Tele-bank. A Black & White I.T.T. 21 inch set with a metal coat hanger hanging out the back as the aerial was put up by me so fell down very often.

Part 16

Swansea by the sea

Like so many before him a young man grow's, he has learned to live at such a young age. There is beauty all around him, the sea, the hills and best of all his young world is coloured by Black and White football scarves. There is an orange sign for the Windsor Café and the bright red roses in Castle Gardens are telling him that the summer at last is here.

There are old fantastic stories describing the treasures you could find in an old Persian bazaar or in an old cave with a door that opens when a magic spell. There is an island near North America where the lost treasure of the Templars is supposed to be buried and for generations gold and diamonds have been mined all over the world. Yet, here in Swansea the tastes and textures, the smells and aromas from all corners of the world can be found on Swansea's streets. The market in the town centre has been built and bombed and built again. It has changed many time's, but it will always be the biggest vault of hidden treasures you could ever wish to visit.

Union Street was as its name suggests a group, a union of shops, pubs and bric- a-brac caves all just waiting to welcome unaware Swansea Jacks and vulnerable strangers in to part them of a schilling or two. Four years very sadly and like many other streets in town Union St even though still busy was a vision of building sitting empty. No rhythms of life disturbed the many old premises falling into disrepair. An example of this being the many rooms, offices and flats that now occupy the voids left by years of squatters destroying all they didn't own above the shops and café's on castle Street.

The war happened night after night but still people of Swansea sing. Our young boy now listens intensely to his Bampi telling him stories of the blitz and his preferred tales of he single handedly scared off the Luftwaffe with his .22 pistol, stories of fishing off the old dock and helping to rebuild the destroyed the market and of course how he and his Mayhill mates were officially the guardians of Swansea during the war.

Swansea survived the War not be shooting back and fighting, not by offering platitudes to silver tongued politicians but by being a family, together. I had a Great aunt, Saffa Lamas who along with my Dad's family came over from Spain in the 1920's and 1930's settling in Swansea. The family run a Chip Shop at the end of Graiglleydd Road, Townhill just before you drop down into Cockett. They welcomed by all around them.

 Just as many other parts of Swansea, Mayhill and Townhill suffered greatly during the war. I remember seeing old photo's of The King and Queen visiting a blitz torn Mayhill during the war.

Now and many years later our young man at the start of our story is a Grandfather himself and as he looks out at his City and for all those who re-built, re-planted and re-designed Swansea after the war he is grateful. Yes the road layouts have changed, the fire station is now occupied by the police and our old school is full of sockless youths with skin tight suits working in an office whilst doing their hair. But and thankfully Joe is still selling his ice-cream, a Mr.Tercerro stills owns and runs La Braseria on Wind Street and you still get the stench of fresh meat and fish in the Market. Some things are not meant to change.

From the Vikings to Cromwell, from an on the run Twm Sion Cati, the Welsh Robin Hood, who forgot the give to the poor bit, and from John Toshak to Rob Brydon Swansea has survived them all. Swansea has been burnt and rebuilt, Hitler's aeroplanes couldn't stop the people of Swansea and now in the first pandemic to hit mankind with any strength in a hundred years or so we are faced with Covid-19. Well all I say to that Mr. Prime Minister is that if you think your rules and English centred rules will stop people who eat cockles and Laver Bread for Breakfast, people who grew up walking everywhere and people who are proud of the Swan their chests and a hero dog on the beach, think again. Swansea Jacks still work, still play and still fish for food and fun. Swansea folk still laugh, still love and most of all still sing. Why I hear you ask Boris?

Swansea is Great
Swansea is Home
Swansea is passion
Swansea is by the Sea.

Part 17

It's 1:00am and again the Tramadol is keeping me awake, I haven't felt this much pain in my back for a long time. As I'm convinced I'm actually growing younger like Benjamin Button it cant be old age knocking the door to come in, can it?

As a kid in Swansea being unwell meant a walk down Waun Wen hill to the doctors' surgery on Carmarthen Rd. The old one looked as if you were entering someone's living room where a stern looking receptionist would take your name and point to whichever door you were to use when it was your turn. Years later, I think I was about 10 years old, the Cwmbwrla Health Centre was opened. This still meant a mammoth walk even if you were on your last legs. We we're patients of Dr. Okane and occasionally Dr. Crooks. Dr. Okane was a joker whilst Dr. Crooks I'm sure was always drunk. My mother's sister Sonia lived on Skinner St, just below Baptist Well so Mam would always get us to call in there on the way home hoping my Uncle Ronald would give us a lift home, if not it was a long walk either up Waun Wen hill or more often than not up the steps next to where the old Tabernacle used to be, up through Colborne Terrace and finally Byron Crescent. After moving up to Creidiol it was even further to moan, sulk and complain. Just opposite where Paul Leonard lived where I think houses are now used to be a shop and a chip shop. I got to know the owner of the chippy in my late teens. Sia Wakasuri was an Iraqi and some of the stories he told me of his life in Iraq at such a turbulent time were frightening. The future leader of Iran Ayatollah Komeinhi was exiled to France but pressure from Saddam Hussein in Iraq saw an uprising that saw the end of the Shah welcoming Komeinhi back. Sia escaped as being a Muslim in a Shia community was dangerous. As I've said in previous passages religious belief in my opinion is the route to all evil. The chip shop we used the most however when I started work so had money to burn was up n Mayhill Shops. 18p for a bag of chips. My first taste of sweet and sour chicken balls was from the Chinese on the top corner, coupled with chips from the chippy, not from the Chinese, my supper on many occasions after a drunken night out was complete. Very often after falling out of the taxi I would Get Mam to walk up with me on the promise of buying her ten fags, we always talked about the days we had both had. Up over Cadwalder Circle then down Allen Street (I think) then up Mayhill Road to the shops. This was a regular occurrence whilst I was still living at home. We had a cat called Darky and he would walk up most of the way with us and wait until we returned purring his excitement to see us coming home. Yan named him after a mob of SAS soldiers who were known as Darkys Mob.

Apart from Mayhill and Sias on Waun Wen the only other chippy was over on Egen at the end of Tegid Road. My favourite however was the old Rossi's Chip Shop down the Hafod, not the one now opposite the Liberty Stadium. I think every day that I should carry on writing these , whatever they are, memories I suppose. I always struggle to think of what to write because I want to write things that my school friends can relate to and remember. Places we all went, things we experienced together and most of all to discuss the bond and friendship I hope and I believe is still there today. We often, via Desmond William Hughes discuss a reunion. It is usually at the wrong time for some and or the wrong place for others. But I really do believe that once all this illness and dark times are away from us, that we have got to make it happen. We the old Dynevor Comprehensive nutters need to organise a date ok with everyone, with plenty of notice in a suitable venue. I certainly for one have forgotten the love and friendship Swansea holds for me, I forgot all about adventures and fights, about kissing girls and playing football, I forgot that even though I wasn't born in Swansea and even though I haven't lived there for a long time, and even though there is pain there is so much more love, when I think of Vera Dawkins and Mary Harris, Christine Leonard and of course my Mam Pauline, I know I'm in Swansea, I'm home

Looking back at old photos of Swansea I smile looking at the Kingsway Roundabout underpass. On shopping days with Mam it was almost an adventure to run up and down the steep walls surrounding the inner circle. It was here you would sometimes come across Tea-Bag sitting with his shopping trolley full of, whatever it was full of, in the entrance to one of the subways would be a busker and I remember on more than one occasion an old gypsy approaching Mam to get her to buy pegs, or lucky trinkets. Mam seemed to enjoy encountering people like this just to challenge them. For example if Jehovah Witnesses knocked the door Mam would invite them in. After 4-5 hours of bible bashing they would leave converted to the Baptist faith or nervous wrecks. The old roundabout was still there when I moved from Swansea and if I recall it was being used as more of a drunken toilet than anything else.

Just off the roundabout was the Wimpy. The McDonalds of its day and a favourite of all kids. Mam had a nephew, my cousin John who as he was same age as Mam were more like siblings. John took us young kids of the family to see the brand new movie Star Trek the Motion Picture in the Castle Cinema afterwards taking us to the Wimpy for burgers and chips. John made a light hearted attempt to look shocked at having to pay for ketchup sachets, joking or not it was clear he wasn't impressed. I remember the old Gas works where Tesco now stands and as I spoke about earlier the terrifying Social Security Office, Oldway House. The bridge going over the main road I think is gone now but I remember John Stefanic and me skateboarding over the bridge to get to the Leisure Centre. I remember Presto's Supermarket and my mate Andy Arntzen worked as a delivery driver for a Photography processing shop close by. One of the girls, Sharon ? We were in school with worked there too. There was C&A clothing store next which was the place I headed for when I was 10 years old when I had £10 from my Dad through the post just so I could buy my first ever new clothes. Everything before were hand me downs from various family members. I bought trousers, a cardigan and shoes. All a lovely shade of brown. I even had enough to buy a new football in the market. The monthly money from my Dad continued and as many of you know most of it was spent on records. At one point I had almost 4000 singles on vinyl. My music was an eclectic assortment. There was Saga, a Canadian rock band ranging then from Madness to Japan and my favourite Franky goes to Hollywood. Martin Henwood got me into the Alarm and I remember Stu Oakley was a great fan of Nick Kershaw. One of my other favourites was Howard Jones who wrote most of Nik Kershaw's hits. David Harris I recall was a great fan of Dame Vera Lynn. Haha.

Being a DJ was my goal and it sort of worked out running clubs both here and in Egypt. Why did I have to grow up?

Olivia my daughter is stuck in lockdown with me and I can see sometimes how much she misses her Mam, how much she longs to be in work with her mates and of course, and I try not to, how much I piss her off daily. Of course we are at a stage where my Dad jokes are shit, my humour generally is shit. My taste in music, food, tv and again humour is shit. I think the only thing she likes about me right now is Jo my girlfriend. Jo and her parents think the world of Olivia. I know she is bored and fed up and of course she is lonely but sometimes, well it hurts. I remember the crap I used to give my Mam, I hated her rules and there weren't many, I hated religion and as a typical teenage cock I hated being skint. As all teenagers do I took it out on my Mam. It's 15 years this year that she died and still every now and then I see something or hear something, and I instantly think, I must tell Mam...then I remember.

It doesn't upset me or anything, what it tells me is that, and thankfully many of your brilliant Mams are going strong, it reminds me our parents were and are still our Mam and Dad, our comfort givers, our teachers and of course our very, very best friends

It's strange but when I chose the theme to these writings I never realised just how Isolation would hurt. Ok I'm not totally isolated but it feels like. As I've said I annoy my daughter constantly and I'm not able to show my beautiful girlfriend how much I love her. Yes I'm feeling down and sorry for myself. I had another round of bloods taken on Friday and had X-ray on my arms. Polymyalgia Rheumatica is more painful than anything I've experienced even breaking my back, I didn't actually feel that. But feeling sorry for myself reminds of my mother. Leaving Hayling Island with a new born baby, me and my brother just 3 years older to come home to Swansea empty handed. Both her parents weren't around, my Grandma had passed away and my Grandpa was in a home , so she had no parents to help. Being a soon to be divorced woman with no money and two kids found her only sadness, more sadness. Her own siblings shunned her. Out of desperation her sister Ruby took us in. We lived on Ceri Road , Townhill. It's strange but as a baby I have a memory of this time. It could just be as someone described but I remember our then next door neighbour . Mable Harris had an old German Shepard called Lana. Lana was huge and apparently to anyone other than Mable quite nasty. Oh and me! This big fearsome dog took a liking to and became very defensive over me. If Mam couldn't get me to sleep they would put me into Lana's lap and she would nurse me to sleep only allowing my Mam or Mable to pick me up. The 3 of us lived in one room of Ruby and my Uncle Herbert's house. Herbert put my mother through hell, he would watch everything she did and I mean everything. If she went out it was timed, what we ate what she wore, everything. We were there 8 months before the Council moved us to Byron Crescent. Mam went through all of this and much more over the years for us. But right now I feel as if I'm falling apart. I am 51 years old and even after my back surgery I've considered myself young at heart and young in body too. Yes I've put on weight, lost weight and never really been ill in my life. Now however I ache all over, my muscles hurt and my joints are really painful, in Lockdown I am working from home but I am bored. I feel I am losing everyone because I can't be the energy boost I normally am. By writing this I realised that isolation is not only being stuck indoors due to Covid, isolation is not only about staying away from other people who could be infected, isolation is in us, in our hearts and minds. I love my daughter without question, I love my girlfriend without conditions. I'm a miserable git I know but tonight, all of you, don't isolate yourself from yourself

Hay on Wye

Part 18

Apologies to all my last chapter was me being thoroughly miserable. I have had a couple of slaps, one from myself and more importantly from Jo, if only with encouraging words. My beautiful girlfriend is my best friend, my confidant and my conscience. Joanne Osborne and I met online just about 19 months ago. I had never looked at ever wanting to get to know someone online but over a couple of weeks we got to know each other little by little. We had agreed to meet to have Sunday Lunch and on the way I was confident and excited and also just a little nervous. I arrived first and as Jo had told me what car she drove I eagerly kept an eye out. Jo arrived and parked a little way away from where I was standing and I watched with anticipation as she walked towards me. Then the moment came when I saw her up close for the first time and my stomach did an almighty flip. Within minutes of meeting I was in love. We have so much in common, so many mutual likes and we both love a good red wine and lots of food.

For the first time in 5 years I celebrated Christmas and when it arrived my birthday. Jo brought life back into me. Like most men of my age I have had many girlfriends, especially when working in nightclubs. But that's a story for another time. For me one of the things I look for when meeting someone is a good sense of humour and the ability to just laugh, be silly and know when it is time to just switch off. Having worked in many parts of the UK and in Egypt and having spent quite a bit of time in Germany I can honestly say, and in my opinion, Welsh women have the best personalities bar none. Jo and I can sit together and just laugh for hours. I remember in school Angela Logan had a brilliant sense of humour and together with Sarah Lewis and Helen Bageridge (sorry about the spelling) the three of them were always laughing.
Some of our teachers in school could have a good laugh also, Mr. Morris our music teacher had quite a funny side, he was also very fiery when the mood found it, and of course Mr. Jowett was a teacher small in stature but a giant in story telling, joking and taking the piss. Many of the teachers had their funny moments, I even think I saw Mr. Deveraux smile once.

Out of us boys we had trouble makers, jokers and absolute nut jobs. We had teachers pets, study freaks and whimp's. But above all we had footballers and fighters, oh yes and some strange sport with an oval shaped ball? I was football and music mad. The best footballers were Carl Dawkins, Michael Wheeler, Michael Burns and Martin Henwood, and of course me, well I think so!
I actually damaged my spine playing football in January 2013.

I played in a 6 a side league in Cardiff and this night it had been snowing all day so even though the pitch had been cleared it froze over very quickly. After diving to make a save two other guys landed on top of me. I couldn't move for a while but kind of shook it off and carried on, very sore but ok. The next day went to work, again very sore, worse the day after and by the Saturday I couldn't stand up. The bottom two discs had snapped into the spine and cut part of the sciatic pathway. Luckily I had Bupa in work so I spent 5 weeks in a 5 star hotel with a pain relief button in one hand tea or coffee button in the other and Sky Sports in front of me. For a good 2 years after my operation and due to the metal now inserted into my spine I set the alarms off in Tesco's. The security guards got to know me. Swansea City was our team, our ambition and our dream. Going to the Vetch as a supporter and a couple of times playing on the hallowed turf was a wish come true. I also have to add a number of times we played at the Vetch wasn't exactly legal, we were young teenagers the gates were open so we went in and played on the pitch. I think it was Mark Hunt that got caught? Up and all around Mayhill we created football pitches everywhere, anywhere it didn't matter, we just had to play football. I'm am determined, however miserable I was yesterday, I am determined this Rheumatism I now have is not going to stop me from playing football again. You never know perhaps I will even see Carl Dawkins goal hanging again one day?

So, we have been in lockdown now for 8 or 9 weeks, I think. Boris and his band of merry men regularly tell us what we are allowed and not allowed to do, unless you are in England. Oh and unless you can work from home but you should now go to work unless you can't go...... You get the picture!

I am not a Conservative supporter, or Labour and Lib Dem for that matter, but I really don't think that whoever is writing Boris's speech notes has any idea of either the real world or how it makes our Prime Minister look. We already knew Boris was more personality than intelligence but give the guy a break and please write him a speech that doesn't put him in such an idiotic position. Now with his right-hand man sort of advisor thingy deciding where and when he wants to visit family members it just put's Boris and the rest of the silver spoon brigade in an even more embarrassing position.

When I started this flog there were 100,00 deaths in the world due to Covid-19, as of today there are 101,00 deaths just in the USA.

As kids in Swansea I suppose we were safely away from the rest of the world. There were terror attacks back then from the IRA and similar minded groups. In our favour was the fact that due to the end of the industrial age of coal and most shipping facilities had left Swansea. Swansea was of no interest to anyone, anywhere except us. Of course there was no internet so no social media and even on TV there was only 3 channels that gave limited news. Whatever was going on in the world in Swansea, in Mayhill on top of the world we didn't see anything.

We only ever knew something was going on when you would walk in your living room and when your eyes had adjusted to the Benson & Hedges fog and you saw all of Mam's friends together you knew something was wrong. Someone was dead, having an affair, in trouble with the coppers or all 3. "Him from number 23 was pissed and he came home and beat the shit out of her so she pissed in his coffee for a month and made him Shepard's pie with a tin of Whiskers", Now that's a poem I want to write about. I think the first time I ever actually watched the news was when a guy called Steven Waldorf was shot 7 times by the Police in London who mistook him for an IRA bomber, and he survived. Pictures glared across our TV's of his bullet riddled Mini. We were lucky.

Swansea, Mayhill and Townhill was home to us and it took care of us keeping harm at a safe distance. We still have a while to go in lockdown and I think thanks to the idiots already ignoring any precautions, I think we are still a long way off ending this nightmare. I will carry on writing and hopefully you will carry on reading. If anything good comes out of this then great, it would be brilliant to see you all and see the grown ups we have all become, in body if not mind. And who knows perhaps be the end of this Carl Dawkins will be able to write a whole sentence without mentioning the word 'Darts' Stay safe xx

It is now 14th September and just as we think we are getting to the end of Covid-19 and its terrible effects, both emotionally and financially. But Oh no! Here it comes again. Personally, I've had enough.

I have been brought off furlough on a part time basis, so I am working 3 days a week. Originally intended to be one day on the phone and two on the road. I had notification yesterday that the company I work for has given me the choice to go out or stay at home due to the current Covid threat.

I watch daily the news both National and Regional and the difference of opinion and the difference in advice is quite frightening. England, Wales, Scotland and Northern Ireland make up Great Britain, the United Kingdom. I think someone needs to explain to our political leaders what United means. Of course, coronavirus not only affects people physically as we know but there must be millions around the world depressed, confused and worried about their financial futures due to the repercussions of lockdown. Many households have lost their income and many people have lost careers and lifestyle's all because of business owners unable to cope with the lack of business caused by lockdown. Where I live near the A470 just below Pontypridd hundreds of homes were decimated by the terrible floods suffered by so many in February and then before a full recovery could be felt by everyone lockdown hit. So many businesses and their premises ruined by water and then destroyed by no custom.

Every day on Facebook there are adverts for insurance and holidays, on TV there are people trying to sell us toothpaste and BMW's and according to most of the media our lives are just continuing as normal.

But, they are not.

Politian's stand in front of the camera's in their Armani suits and multi-million-pound education and bank balances and it is more than obvious that in reality they haven't a clue how the normal, whatever that is, normal family actually live.

Above Builth Wells

Mumbles from Nicander Parade

Part 19

When I started this writing, I didn't know where I wanted to go with this work. When putting the work onto Facebook the responses received by my friends, the anecdotes and the memories shared was something I never expected. It was brilliant. Just like so many of you, my friends I have had pain and struggles and just like so many others I try to make my future a little better. I still make mistakes, I still struggle with certain aspects, I hate the dates of my son's birthday and death. My job has my driving around many beautiful parts of Wales to see my customers and is something I love doing. Most of the photographs included in this work have been taken on my visits to customers in various parts of Wales, on lunch breaks of course.

Like so many others I am scared a little about what sort of future we are heading into, more for my beautiful daughter and her peer's. Jo my girlfriend has two children still in school and trying to work out what sort of world will be around when they leave school is worrying. What has happened?

My Grandfather came from Spain to Swansea for a better and fruit full life. Throughout time there has always been that special place to go in the world. Where will our children or grandchildren go? The whole world is in trouble. Government leaders throughout the world have agendas and greed, they have Gods that don't exist but whom they worship, they have minions who only see a figure not a person.

Donald trump is a living cartoon character, so childish in his speeches so liberal with his personal views and yet so misleading with his opinions and views. North Korea has a despot leader without any charisma and European leaders are just led by Mrs. Merkel in Germany. For us, well we have Boris!

I don't blame him for anything, we all know Prime Ministers don't make any real decisions, it's the advisors and so-called experts who tell him what to say. Unfortunately for Boris he hasn't got the professional tools to carry it off. He is like the scruffy unkempt swot in school who is excellent at Chemistry but the boy who can't get a girlfriend because his mother still dresses him. He is awkward and uncomfortable and, as much as I dislike the political heads we have right now, I think his honest ignorance makes him the best person for the job. I think Peers Morgan should take over the world.

Ffochriw

There are stories on the news about Covid tests not being done to the expected level, tests are not being completed properly. Why not?

Multi-Millionaire Professional footballers can get a test whenever they want, is it because they can pay privately?

How much does a human life cost?

There are so many movies about post-apocalyptic battles that strangely but unnervingly resemble the world we are living in today. Yet we still look for the positive, we still long for that one thing that makes our day liveable.

As kids in Swansea we lived with hardship, it was normal for us but as times have changed how many of us lived it would be considered real poverty today. Trying to explain what a Tele bank black and white TV was to my daughter is like explaining the Ikea instructions for building a cabinet, almost impossible. The very idea of putting first 10p coins then 50p coins into a meter attached to the TV is baffling, and shameful. We had our first colour TV when I was 16 or 17 years old. Mam just couldn't afford the TV licence. We never had a phone in the house and indeed only had a fridge when I was about 8 or 9.

Of course, nothing we had was new in fact normally it was because a member of my Mam's family was throwing something out to move brand new in. We were the family charity case without doubt. If Covid lockdown has taught me anything it is to be humble. I have stopped trying to please everyone, well, I am trying. Just like Jo my beautiful girlfriend, we both try and be everything for and to everyone else and most of the time our time together is if we possibly fit each other in around lifts, shopping and of course taxi-ing. Jo is constantly on to me to start looking after myself properly. The pain killers I am on have totally removed my taste buds and my appetite. During lockdown whilst most working from home have put on weight I have actually lost almost 2 stone. I need to lose weight I know.

What has kept me going through all this though is humour. I think I'm a great comedian which I'm sure Olivia my daughter will totally poo on. Jo's Dad Rob and I get on great and we have something of a joke rivalry going on, I'm convinced I'm winning! Then it's reading posts from Carl Dawkins who can make any subject sound like a comedy sketch. Martin Henwood and his Delia Smith cookery tips and of course David Harris with his ever-changing hairstyle. I enjoy the humour in Mrs. Browns Boys and anything with Peter Kay and of course Jo and I love watching Gavin and Stacey. The one program however which has personally given me so much is After-life.

I was never a fan of Ricky Gervais until Jo introduced me to After-life, the story of a newspaper reporter dealing with the death of his wife from cancer who was his lover, his friend and his soul mate. He also has to deal with a motley crew of work colleagues, an over friendly Post-man and a prostitute best friend. Whereas there is sadness and quite a bit of irony and wit there is also a great deal of comedy. Gervais wrote this himself and I have to call it genius. It has had me crying with laughter and tears rolling down my face with the painful hurt he feels over the loss of his wife.

So, what I am trying to get over is that Covid/lockdown or however you name the current situation we are living in, is that from being a struggling kid with no money, no real prospects and no idea of how to live, just like millions of others I have learnt to live. Nothing has prepared us for what we are enduring now. No event in childhood, no painful news growing up and no death of a passing loved one could ever have got us ready for the pain so many are feeling today.

If as Donald Trump suggests Covid is man-made there has to be justice. If governments around the world could have controlled and saved lives much better than they have there needs to be justice. If and only if it gets worse to the levels of the height of lockdown then all of our leaders need to put people first and not their own political agendas.

Keep Walking

To all the heroes waiting
I salute you,
For all the women praying
I support you,
For each and every dreamer tonight
I encourage you.

For where there is you
There is hope,
Where there is love
There is sunshine,
Where there is a dream
There is a future.
If there is a road, walk on it
If there is a sea, swim in it
If there is a sky, fly in it
If there is a tune, then sing!
Always move forward.

To the commander who has won a battle
We are humbled
For the child who has beaten a cancer
We are thankful
For a nation standing up to tyranny
We are proud of you
We must all walk
We must learn to run
We can all swim and fly
We must all keep dreaming

For those that cannot walk
I will carry you
For those that dare not run
We will support you
For those who cannot swim or fly
We will help to make your dreams come true.
If there is a road, walk on it
If there is a sea, swim in it
If there is a sky, fly in it
If there is a tune, then sing!
Always move forward.
Always Keep walking

Ffochriw

Lift the Blade

The cross you sign across your chest
The look you give your follower
All you see is a golden coin
For God they become a borrower

No matter god you choose to serve
No matter who you follow
Putting your faith in a faceless fool
Will fill you full of sorrow

A golden cross and wooden pew
A man dressed all in white
A congregation of besotted idiots
All searching for a light

Looking up and over you all
Ambition starts to fade
The only help the holy man gives
Is the lift of the holy blade.

Thank You and please stay safe

I am David Kimmeran Aleman

All words written are mine as are the opinions and views given

All poetry is written and owned by me

All photographs are taken and owned by me

I would like to say a huge Thank you to all my friends who have supported this work and acknowledge this work

Thanks also go to Joanne Osborne my girlfriend

And of course, Olivia Luckwell my daughter

Both for their love and support.

Thebeardedpoet88@gmail.com